...ege

Sixty ...

D0714973

Leif Frimann Anisdahl · Kay Atkins
Arthur Baker · Stuart Barrie · Alan Blackman
Jef Boudens · Jeroen Boudens
Philip Bouwsma · Robert Boyajian · Gunnlaugur SE Briem
Lida Lopes Cardozo · Rick Cusick · Sidney Day
Timothy Donaldson · Marc Drogin · Ward Dunham
Jean Evans · Henri Friedlaender · Peter Halliday
David Harris · Michael Harvey
Jost Hochuli · Karlgeorg Hoefer · Lothar Hoffmann
David Howells · Nancy Ouchida Howells · Pam Jones
Torfi Jónsson · Jerry Kelly · David Kindersley
Jean Larcher · Lilly Lee · Chuck Lehman · Harry Meadows
Karina Meister · Merilyn Moss · Pat Musick
Anne Yokosakamaki Okimoto · Ronald Parsons
Leonid Pronenko · David Quay · Mohammed Said Saggar
Hans Schmidt · Werner Schneider · Paul Shaw
John Smith · Bonnie Spiegel · John Stevens · Alan Swanson
Villu Toots · Mark Van Stone · Jovica Veljović
Julian Waters · Sheila Waters · Eleanor Winters
Berthold L. Wolpe · James L. Wood
Lili Cassel Wronker · Hermann Zapf
Gudrun Zapf-von Hesse

Sixty Alphabets

Selected & introduced by
Gunnlaugur SE Briem

THAMES AND HUDSON

Photographic acknowledgments

Dr Leila Avrin, 118; F. C. Buxton, 44; Afien Kruizinga, 76; Edward
Leigh, 28; Heidi Maasikmets, 106; Samfoto, Oslo, 8.
Drawing of Anne Yokosakamaki Okimoto by Lefty Fontenrose.
Drawing of Lilly Lee reproduced by permission of John Springs.
Cover photo by John Myers

Text set in 10pt Diotima

Printed and bound in Great Britain by
R. J. Acford Ltd, Chichester, Sussex.

INTRODUCTION

It isn't easy to explain what attracts some people to letterforms with such joy and fury. Most people can't tell typing from printing and the latest figures on illiteracy suggest that we should be grateful, while we can, that they can read at all.

In comparison to details of such other callings as, say, keeping rabbits, small particulars of the alphabet can easily become an obsession. I often think of Thomas Cobden-Sanderson, a remarkable man and a bookbinder of distinction, as he stood on Hammersmith Bridge in the dark, throwing the printing type of the Doves Press into the Thames. This was a crime of passion and has a comical side that the decades often give to such things. But I can see him, heart pounding, full of earnest purpose, as he puts his beloved type to rest. He was not about to wonder, as the song wonders about the lady, who might be kissing her now.

I could name a few things that I'd like to throw into the Thames myself in the shadow of night. But my reasons would not be as pure as his. My motive wouldn't be love.

Lettering people disagree over everything. They argue about the very purpose of the alphabet, which is as good a point for a fight as any.

Some people say that letters exist to be read and therefore the things that interfere with legibility should be discouraged. (This is a bit like saying that the purpose of liquor is to get you drunk. If it were right, people would swig metal polish and the farmers of Cognac, Burgundy and Champagne grow potatoes.)

The alphabet, the argument goes, should be a well-mannered servant who quietly carries messages from author to reader. This is sometimes true: it is just what we need in the telephone directory. Fortunately, the world still has some other uses for letters as well; otherwise this book and the exhibition with which it is associated would have been difficult to arrange. We celebrate the alphabet for other reasons than legibility. We enjoy all the passion and the fury and could hardly have more fun without breaking the furniture.

The alphabet has a style for every need. For dignity, the style of Roman inscriptions is unsurpassed. To attempt the limits of human skill, people have decorated letters almost beyond recognition in some of the world's greatest manuscript books. More than a code for text, the alphabet has developed through the centuries into a splendid medium of expression. Even the greeting card with pink pigs from your friend Henry had a printed message that was made to look silly expressly to match his sense of humour. I think it's marvellous and I don't think any permanent damage was done to our heritage.

As long as people seem to like letters made of soap bubbles, the world can't be all bad. A few colleagues of mine have been driven to despair over some lovely letters with snow on top that are used in winter advertising. These things did not come about by accident. No designer consciously decided to forfeit his reputation and go down in history wearing a fool's cap. They were made because people wanted them and it is because people still do that they are used every year as the weather gets cold.

The alphabet is as much an element of human civilization as our cathedrals and railway lines. It is part of our lives, like the clothes we wear and the songs we sing. We make letters that express moods; we have given them a tone of voice. Like painting, they involve colour and composition. Like music they have a range of emotions. To some of us, they are our songs.

Even if we agree that expression is a part of the alphabet, and agree again that it sometimes comes before legibility, we still have many things to disagree over. One thing that divides people is the approach. They ask what kind of lettering is permissible in polite society. What kind of expression can the common man be trusted with?

One view, especially liked by amateurs, is that the only legitimate way of using the alphabet for expression is to imitate medieval methods. This means that you should write with a feather. You should work on vellum if you can afford it, on hand-made paper if not (even if it only differs from comparable machine-made paper in the direction of the fibres). You should approach the job with reverence and possibly make your own ink. All this is said to be justified by regarding writing, illuminating, and lettering as medieval crafts.

Most of the reasoning about the traditions of lettering also applies to plumbing, which has work practices that go back many centuries. The traditional methods of elbow soldering may have been abandoned and some plumbing amateurs probably deplore this. But we still get the water in and the sewage out. It works. What matters in a piece of lettering, too, is whether it works. For romantic reasons it may be crucial that the egg in the tempera was laid by a free-range hen. More important, however, is what the thing looks like.

The people who rely on tradition in all things alphabetical often find it a heavy crutch. They make a virtue of imitation and take few chances. Their work is impersonal and much of it might come from the same pen. It is dull because they have nothing to say except the obvious.

As lettering is a task full of uncertainty, loosely argued opinions are defended with an intensity that they do not deserve. It is a labour of love; otherwise people would not treat each other so badly over points of little consequence. On occasion, it seems to inspire feelings that in earlier times were reserved for heretics. But, then, some aspects of modern lettering are largely a matter of belief and a few of the ideas that support it not only defy logic but seriously discourage common sense. In lettering, remarkably little has been formulated of clear thought that can be put directly to use. Many people who make splendid letters run into trouble over numerals and are defeated by punctuation.

There is great joy in the perfect spacing of an apostrophe. Through the centuries, most of the problems in fitting lettershapes together have been solved by printers and typographers, often very gracefully. Their work is there for all to see, but not often put to use in lettering. Instead, schisms come about over technique. Matters of taste turn into a heresy. People are tempted to grab destiny by the throat and deal with dissent by bell, book and candle.

To outsiders, this looks hilarious. But making fun of earnest people is not fair. They see a noble tradition defenceless in an unchartered, treacherous world. They want to protect what they love. If they are a bit vague about parts of it, then so are we all, I suppose, on some subjects. I am convinced, for instance, that the Earth turns around the Sun but I'd have a hard time proving it. If some of my friends allow their tempers to rise over an irresponsible serif, that is their privilege. If they want to make gesso by slaking plaster, rather than buying gilding base in a tube, they probably have their reasons.

As obsessions go, lettering is a wonderful thing. Anybody with a pen and an idea can have a go.

Despite all claims to the contrary, I believe there's hope for the world yet. I have two reasons. One is the survival quality of the alphabet. In the long run, neither individual nor institutional silliness seems to have made serious mischief. The other reason is that it never seems to stop fascinating people. We make letters that have already been made through the ages in unthinkable numbers. Not only do we work on a style. Much of our delight is in modifying and redefining it so that it reflects who we are.

I have trust in people and believe that in the long haul, good sense will prevail. Until it does, watching the fights is no end of fun.

Leif Frimann Anisdahl

Anisdahl/Christensen AS
Design & Kommunikasjon
Professor Dahls gate 37
0353 Oslo 3

Anisdahl was born in 1937 in Drammen, Norway. On leaving school he served four years' apprenticeship in typography. He subsequently attended the Graphic College in Copenhagen (1960-62) before working as a designer at the Gutenberghus, Copenhagen (1962-3) and at Penguin Books in London (1963). Returning to Norway he became a designer at the Gyldendal Publishing House, Oslo, and from 1966 ran his own design studio in Oslo with Carl T. Christensen. His work has been represented in various publications and on Norwegian stamps and banknotes.

Calligraphic Letters are written with Passion

8

Kay Atkins

515 Spring Street
Newport
Rhode Island 02840

A native of Seattle, Washington, and a 1963 graduate of Marylhurst College in Oregon, Kay Atkins' first experience with calligraphy was with Sister Lloya Mary and Lloyd Reynolds. What started twenty years ago as a suitable appointment for a woman's education became a way of life with a Master's in Calligraphy from Southeastern Massachusetts University in 1982.

Kay lives in Newport, Rhode Island, with three college-bound children and two dogs; she enjoys working in a community of unusual writing artists. Her days are spent working at the Redwood Library, her evenings teaching calligraphy at The Swinburne School and doing freelance work. Her spare time has been spent in completing a book entitled *Italic Exemplars of the Sixteenth Century*, which is being published by David Godine Inc.

This unlikely combination of loose, slightly flourished italic majuscules and bookish, unflourished minuscules is what has evolved as my personal handwriting. Whatever it is or isn't suits me, for I take great pleasure in using it for everything from business communiqués and shopping lists to unruly notes to friends.

abcdefghijklmnopqrstuvwxyz

Arthur Baker

Woods Road
Germantown
New York 12526

Arthur Baker is the author of twenty books on calligraphic art and instruction. He has had one-man shows of his work in London, Iceland, New York and St Louis. He enjoys designing and flying paper aeroplanes, and is the author of a book titled *Full color Paper Airplanes that fly*, published by Dover. He counts as one of his greatest achievements having never been invited to teach a workshop at a national calligraphy conference.

27 august 1965

Stuart Barrie

41 Ann Street
Edinburgh EH4 1PL

Stuart Barrie was born in Edinburgh in 1925. He was trained at the Edinburgh College of Art under Nora Paterson from 1947 to 1951, and has been a lecturer at the College in Lettering and Graphic Design since 1957. He became a member of the Society of Scribes and Illuminators in 1958, and of the Society of Industrial Artists and Designers in 1964.

His work has been shown at the exhibitions of the Society of Industrial Artists and Designers and at the Annual Exhibitions of the Society of Scottish Artists; examples have also been reproduced in various publications, most recently in *Modern Scribes and Lettering Artists* and in the catalogue *Calligraphy '84*.

This alphabet is related to some designs I have worked on in the past; the designs were of lettering for reproduction with decorated terminations. There is probably no real application for this design except as a decoration. Long words, for example, would be unsuccessful in the recognizability/legibility factor vital to serious alphabet designs, i.e. the ones which deal with the assembly of text and the design of word shapes in *all* combinations of letters (e.g. type design).

In general, one of the only precepts that I cling to, is that *lettering is an act of drawing* as well as of communication, and that 'good' lettering is an art rather than a craft. Lettering should fulfil its function with sensitivity, originality, and, if possible, beauty.

Alan Blackman

1125 Shrader Street
San Francisco
California 94117

Alan Blackman began his study of the lettering arts when most present-day scribes were still in their cradles. He has now been teaching it almost as long. He lives, works and studies in San Francisco, where he is an active member of the Friends of Calligraphy.

Paramount among the inspirations in his life is his son, Stephen, who resides in the UK. He is an admirer of many diverse elements of the German-speaking cultures: the art of Paul Klee; the writings of Schiller, Rilke, Günter Grass and Siegfried Lenz; the operas of Wagner and Richard Strauss; and the calligraphy of Rudolf Koch, Hoefer, Neugebauer and Burgert. He is fond of inscriptional Greek lettering of the Stocheidon period.

The letters for this composite Greco-Roman alphabet were written with a bamboo pen on bond paper for reproduction on a Toshiba BD-7815 copy machine. The original writing is 3.4 cm high.

Jef Boudens

Abdijbekestraat 53
B-8200 Brugge

Born in Bruges in 1926, Jef Boudens is a self-taught calligrapher. Professor of the Art School in Ghent and of the Academy of Arts in Roeselare, he is the author of books on calligraphy and letter design (his special interest). He has travelled widely and collaborated with editors in Europe, the USA and the Soviet Union. One of his five children is a letter sculptor.

Jeroen Boudens

Heidelbergstraat 106
8021 Loppem
Belgium

Jeroen Boudens was born in Bruges in 1956 and studied reprophotography at the Higher Institute for Graphical Instruction at Ghent. On the successful completion of his studies he trained and served apprenticeship with various blacksmiths before establishing himself as an independent artist in wrought iron. After five years he began to accept additional work in a graphic publishing house; he has also designed several pieces of furniture and a wood-burning stove. Design has remained his favourite hobby. He is married with two children, Joàchim and Hezeke.

This alphabet is not 'calligraphy' as such, but just twenty-six letters that form a unity. My intention was to sell the alphabet to a firm producing rub-down letters, for use as a company logo or in advertising campaigns. The combination of some of the letters could lead to playful and pleasant results, while remaining legible and meaningful.

20

AAAAAAABBB
CCCCCDEEEFF
GGGHHHHHI
JJJJKKKLLL
MMNNOOP
QRRRRRSTU
UUXYZZ
1234567890
?!?.., ŒÆ

Philip Bouwsma

18 Beacon Road
Bethany
Connecticut 06525

Born in 1948, Philip Bouwsma was engaged in graduate studies in Ancient History at Berkeley before becoming a professional calligrapher in 1971. He worked in the San Francisco area and New York City before moving to rural Connecticut in 1978, where he lives with his wife and two daughters. Since then he has concentrated on historical research and on abstract calligraphy and sculpture. He has completed a book in collaboration with Arthur Baker, and has published several articles. Bouwsma is the first to apply the principles of Western calligraphy to abstract sculpture in steel, bronze and other materials. He has conducted numerous workshops and exhibited widely in an effort to promote understanding of historical calligraphy and its significance in contemporary art.

'Roman Alphabet'
Calligraphy is the basis of much Oriental art, but in the Western tradition it has been regarded as merely functional, a tool in the service of language. In order to make the viewer see calligraphic letters as classic forms in the highest tradition of Western art, it is necessary to disarm the reading mode, in which the reader simply scans the page for pattern recognition without becoming sensuously engaged in the forms, and force the viewer to come to terms with the movement and harmony of the strokes. This is the purpose of presenting artistic calligraphy in the form of alphabets.

This process is taken a step further if the letters are taken out of the context of legibility altogether so that they must be viewed as abstract forms; and another step toward abstraction is achieved if they are taken out of the realm of two dimensions and projected into three-dimensional space, either by perspective or in sculpture. Once they are rendered absolutely useless, then they can only be considered as art. The formal harmony of the roman capitals, achieved (as Arthur Baker has shown) not through Euclidian geometry or static proportion but through harmony of the angle changes of the broad pen, sustains a complexity and variety in three dimensions which reflect the dynamic symmetry of nature.

22

Robert Boyajian

511 Third Avenue
New York
New York 10016

Robert Boyajian is a freelance lettering artist, designer and calligrapher with over thirty years experience in the advertising field.

This alphabet was quickly and freely written (at the first attempt) with a Philip Bouwsma pen. The corners of the pen are slit so I can add a flourish as I write without fear of the pen catching or spluttering.

   I enjoy working with letters and see each job as a challenge and a chance to express creativity.

24

Gunnlaugur SE Briem

21 Shepherd's Bush Road
London W6 7LX

Briem is a designer and lives in London. He has of late taken an active interest in the introduction of italic handwriting in his native Iceland. With the Second Hand Press and the Appleman Gallery he makes impossible ideas into futile reality.

Juan de Yciar's rotunda of 1548 was a distant inspiration for my piece. It is an old friend.

I've never worked much with southern gothic. Lovely as it can be, I have never seen in it the opportunities for irresponsibility that make some other styles amusing company. It looks at the world with a steady gaze from large hymnal pages, forgiving of our follies but hardly tempted to join in. My favourites have been styles that you might associate with acrobats and painted ladies, such as ragged square caps and flamboyant italics.

Then for some reason Juan de Yciar's woodcut started occurring to me at odd moments; it wouldn't leave me alone. I sat down and made some sketches but that was not enough. I kept thinking about it. I tried it out on a rigid grid and bashed it about a lot. It was less trouble designing the letters than getting the frames where I wanted them. The piece took about a week, from the first sketches to cutting the wood, mahogany veneer on chipboard: filthy stuff.

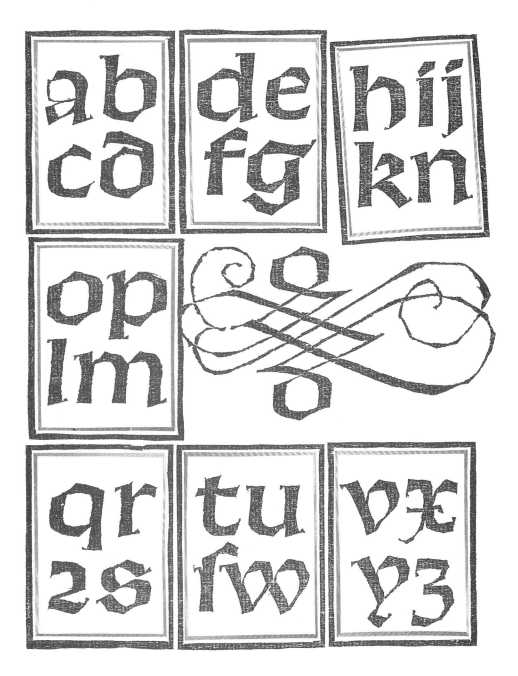

Lida Lopes Cardozo

152 Victoria Road
Cambridge CB4 3DZ

Lida Lopes Cardozo was born in 1954 in Holland. She has *no* diplomas, *no* awards, one child, also a cat and a rook, and works as much as she can (and there is always more) in stone, glass or on paper or computer. David Kindersley and she run a workshop in Cambridge with four, sometimes five 'lettermakers'.

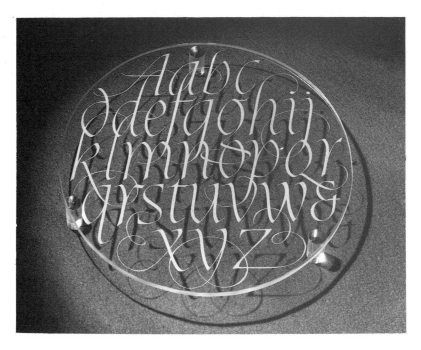

'Alphabet Roundel'

The name of my piece is 'Alphabet Roundel'. It was first made in glass. That glass roundel I still have myself. One of the few things I got sentimental over and do not really want to sell. (Every woman has her price though!)

Rick Cusick

11116 West 71st Terrace
Shawnee
Kansas 66203

Rick Cusick attended San Joaquin Delta College in Stockton, California, and Art Center College of Design in Los Angeles. He is an Associate Design Manager at Hallmark Cards in Kansas City, Missouri, and teaches Editorial Publication Design at the University of Kansas in Lawrence, Kansas. He also acts as Editorial and Design Consultant for TBW Books of Woolwich, Maine. For TBW he compiled and edited *With Respect . . . to RFD* (1978), an appreciation of calligrapher Raymond F. DaBoll; *Straight Impressions* (1979), essays and calligraphy by Lloyd J. Reynolds; provided the calligraphy for *The Proverbial Bestiary* (1982), with drawings by Warren Chappell; and collaborated with his wife, Richie, on *The Ink & The Paper* (1984), a fable inspired by Leonardo da Vinci. His work has appeared in numerous exhibitions and publications.

Untitled
An attempt to explore the graphic possibilities (and visually represent the sound and energy) of the International Morse Code.

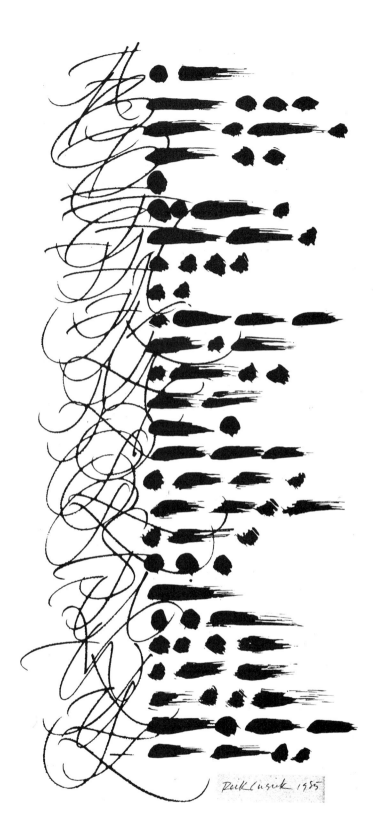

Sidney Day

1B Desborough Drive
Tewin Wood
Welwyn
Hertfordshire AL6 0HQ

Sidney Day is happily married with three children, lives in Hertfordshire and spends some time in north Norfolk. Following four years' service in the Royal Air Force he studied graphic design and printmaking at Hornsey College of Art until gaining the NDD and ATD in 1952. He subsequently worked in graphics as a freelance and taught part-time at art colleges before becoming a full-time Senior Lecturer in Graphics/Typography at Middlesex Polytechnic in 1976. He is currently Course Leader of the three-year BA (Hons) in Graphic Design.

Following a wide range of activity in his early career, he came to the late conclusion (at over 40) that calligraphy would make an excellent specialist interest. He studied with Dorothy Mahoney, who had been a pupil of Edward Johnston and who had continued to teach the subject at the Royal College of Art after his death in 1944.

He has some regrets that even more spare time is not available for this firm calligraphic interest.

'A Bestiary Caroline'

The alphabet is firmly based upon English tenth-century Caroline, best exemplified in the work of the scribe who wrote BM Harley 2904. Even after many years of acquaintance with the minuscule, one is constantly discovering new subtleties about its construction. The Italian Renaissance in the fifteenth century produced two related humanist scripts derived from Caroline letterforms, namely roman and italic. The latter demanded fewer pen lifts and produced increased fluency together with some lateral compression.

The drawings are added because it is felt that an alphabet can only be seen to work properly when individual letterforms are used in conjunction with others. An attempt has been made to relate the pictorial matter to the lithographic printmaking process used.

Armadillo has a covering of horny plates or bands connected by flexible skin enabling it to roll up in a ball for defence · The nine banded species found in South & Central America feeds mainly on insects ·

Buffalo Amongst the largest species of cattle, the water buffalo is found in Asia and parts of Europe as domesticated animal and is becoming much rarer in the wild ·

Camel The Bactrian Camel, found in the wild in the Gobi Desert & elsewhere has two functional toes which are supported by expanded pads for walking on sand ·

Deer Native to India and Sri Lanka, the Axis Deer is regarded as the most attractive of India's eight species · Its local name 'chital' means 'spotted deer' ·

Elephant Its most conspicuous feature is a long flexible trunk, an elongation of the nose · The African Elephant, found south of the Sahara is distinguished from its Asiatic counterpart mainly by its large ears ·

Fox Cunning and resourceful, the fox manages to survive in many places · He is most active at night when he kills small mammals (field voles & rabbits) for food and lives in a family group ·

Giraffe The male giraffe grows to 18ft tall and usually lives with a small herd on the African savanna from the arid west to the Sudan where acacia trees grow · East African species have an extra pair of horns ·

Hedgehog Our only spiny mammal, the hedgehog has been around the countryside for centuries & feeds mainly on beetles, caterpillars and earthworms · It hibernates in winter in a nest of leaves ·

Iguana Of the 700 species the common iguana is best known and lives amongst the trees of South American tropical forests · It has teeth on the inner side of the jaw, scaly crest on its back & can move swiftly ·

Jaguar The largest carnivore of the South American forest, the jaguar can weigh up to 250 lb and grow to over 8ft in length · It usually preys on forest animals like peccaries, agoutis and deer ·

Kangaroo Found mainly in open grassland throughout Australia, the Red Kangaroo has a small head, large ears & long hind limbs and feet · Its long tail is used as a prop and to maintain balance when leaping ·

Lemur A tree dwelling animal distantly related to the monkey, the lemur has flourished in Madagascar for millions of years · It lives mainly on fruit and leaves but some species will eat insects ·

Mole The mole is some 6 inches in length has big heavily clawed front feet for tunnelling & a silky black furred body · It lives under ground in a tunnel complex and eats earthworms ·

Numbat This banded ant & termite eater is found in open forest and scrub in the west and south of Australia · It is a red-brown colour with seven or so white bands and a long tail ·

Okapi The okapi is found deep in the congo forest where it was only discovered by Europeans in the early part of this century · Dark chestnut in colour it has white stripes on legs and flank ·

Pig Commonly kept in back yards, the pig was a bountiful provider for the whole household · The Pietrain, a lean dark spotted species has been bred in Belgium during this century ·

Quokka A stockily built marsupial about 2ft in length which inhabits the scrub and swampy areas of western Australia's offshore islands · It rests during the day and emerges to feed at night ·

Rhinoceros The white rhino can weigh up to 3½ tons and has a longer head and larger ears than the black species · It has a square upper lip and is a grazing animal ·

Sheep The original British sheep were small and hardy and tough hill breeds like the Whitefaced Dartmoor are descended from them · Its long fleece is somewhat unusual in hill varieties ·

Tiger The largest of all the big cats the male Tiger can weigh up to 400 lb and measure 9ft from head to tail · The main populations are confined to India and South East Asia ·

Uintatherium A now extinct large American herbivore some 12 ft long and built like a modern Rhinoceros · It lived some 30-50 million years ago in the Eocene epoch ·

Viper Distributed widely in Britain and found on farmland, moor land, in hedgerows and woods · The Viper or Adder is Britain's commonest Snake & the only one that is poisonous ·

Walrus The one species is found in the Pacific or the Atlantic but that in the Pacific is larger and has nostrils placed higher on the muzzle · A 2½ in thick layer of blubber insulates it from the cold ·

Exmoor Pony Belongs to the Northern pony family, a tough species that is capable of surviving in Arctic regions · Its thick wiry coat provides excellent insulation during the most severe winters ·

Yak The wild Yak still exists in Tibet and North West China but has been domesticated in Tibet for centuries · The wild species survives on the highest plateau at between 1500 & 1700 ft ·

Zebra Both wildebeeste and zebra compete for grazing on the Serengeti plain in East Africa, the most common zebra being the Burchell's · Large herds are made up of individual family units ·

This alphabet, the Caroline or Carolingian minuscule, named after the Emperor Charlemagne (742 - 814) is derived from earlier continental writing hands developed from Roman influences · This period which involved the revival of learning and reform of writing, covered roughly the years 780 - 1100 AD · The new script was introduced at the west Frankish monastery of Tours and was supervised by Alcuin of York who subsequently developed throughout Europe, the best examples written in the late 10th century by English scribes · These can be seen in the British Museum manuscripts · Barley 607 AD and 2904 upon which Edward Johnston based his foundational hand and from which modern classical typefaces have descended ·

Timothy Donaldson

5 Stanley Villas
Runcorn
Cheshire

Timothy Donaldson was tired, at 22, of being on the dole, so he bought himself a set of ladders and started cleaning windows. An interest in drawing and a desire to improve his handwriting started him thinking about earning a living as a signwriter, and he now runs a sign company. As a self-taught calligrapher he has participated in various exhibitions and works for a wide variety of clients in all sorts of media, from silkscreen printing to glass engraving. He is now 25.

'Quartet'
This spontaneous working method is the one I enjoy most as I don't get much chance to use it in my everyday work. I work fast because it is the only way to produce such letterforms and hand-made paper is used as it provides the most responsive surface for the movement of the tool. The pen is the cheapest I own; it consists of a bit of matchbox stuffed into a dried plant stem. The forms are unretouched.

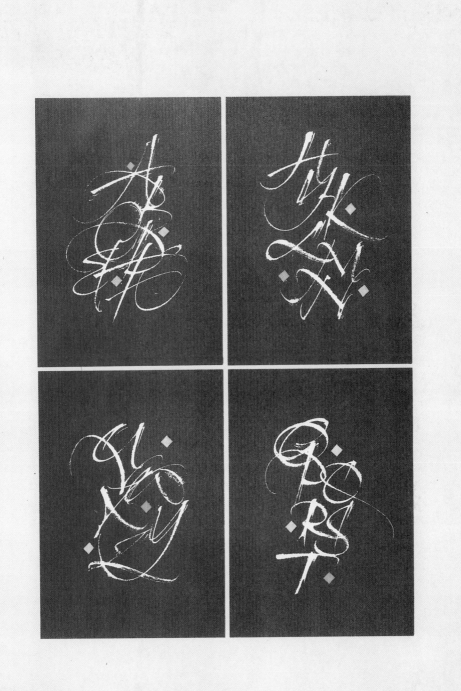

Marc Drogin

74 Court Street
Exeter
New Hampshire 03833

Marc Drogin has a love for the Middle Ages and can be found in England and America teaching its scripts, lecturing on its scribes' travails and idiosyncrasies, and writing on both. He is the author of *Medieval Calligraphy – Its History & Technique, Anathema! Medieval Scribes and the History of Book Curses* and *Yours Truly, King Arthur*, and is now at work on *Biblioclasm!*, a study of the mythical origins and magic powers of the alphabet and ancient books. A cartoonist as well, Drogin invariably finds whimsy in the past and mirth in things medieval.

ABCDE
FGHIKL
MNOPQ
RSTV
XYZ

IN ROMAN TIMES MOST OF THE
OF MANKIND RESTED ON PAPYRUS.
ROMANS FOUND THAT THE AROMA
EUPHORIC. INNUMERABLE MANU-
AS ROMANS, HAVING ONCE READ A BOOK,
ALAS, ENJOYED IT AGAIN.

HISTORY AND LITERATURE
AND NONE TOO SAFELY, FOR THE
OF BURNING PAPYRUS WAS
SCRIPTS THEN WERE LOST
WENT BACK AND,

Marc Drogin · 1985
BIBLIOCLASM!

Ward Dunham

Gargoyle Graphics
PO Box 33 0138
San Francisco
California 94133 0138

Ward Dunham is an artist/bohemian who lives and works in San Francisco. He has been a student of calligraphy since 1964, when he discovered the broad-edged tool in Viet-Nam, where he was a Special Forces adviser. In 1974 he began to narrow his calligraphic horizons to the Gothic period in northern Europe, using just black and one colour, usually vermilion. Dunham is a founding member of the Society of Scribes (New York City), the New Orleans Calligraphers Association and the Friends of Calligraphy (San Francisco). He exhibits, teaches and travels widely.

Jean Evans

142 Garden Street
Cambridge
Massachusetts 02138

Jean Evans grew up in South Carolina. After earning an AB in Art/Art History at Queens College, Charlotte, North Carolina, she moved to Cambridge, Massachusetts, and coached the Radcliffe Tennis Team. Her interest in calligraphy, graphic design and type design has evolved through workshops, exhibitions, conferences, travel and jobs. She has recently been associated with the Brownstone Group, doing calligraphy and graphic design, and currently works with Bitstream Inc. designing type.

This alphabet began in 1979 as an A to Z listing for the New England Book Show Directory; it was also used for headings in various sections of the book.

 The alphabet shown here is a more robust 1984 update of that original. It was written with my trusty popsicle stick nipped off at a proper 60° angle and executed in a manner perhaps more Oriental than anything else, in that I did the characters over and over again until I felt I was 75 years old and had almost gotten them 'right'.

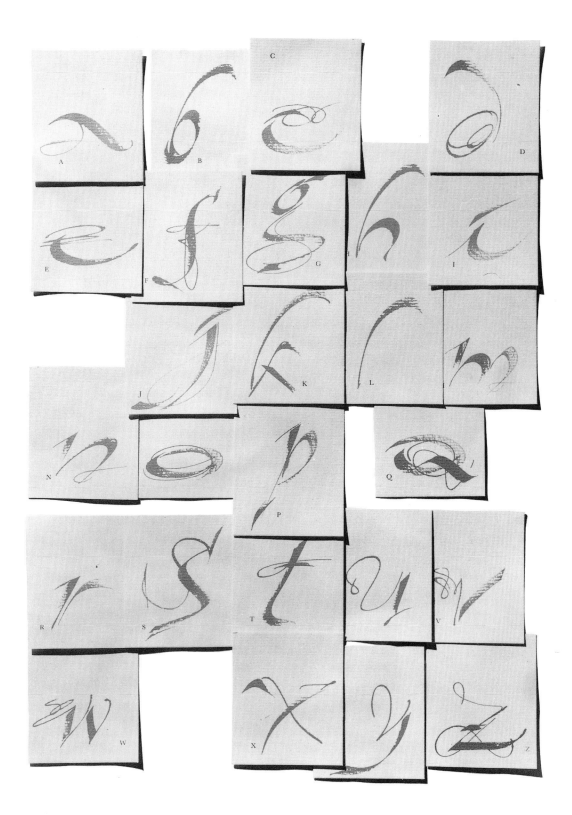

Henri Friedlaender

Sderot Ha-Rishonim 14
Motza Illit
95743 Jerusalem

Henri Friedlaender's early childhood was spent in France, since when he has divided his time between Germany (1910-32), Holland (1932-50) and Israel (1950-).

'Calligraphy' (i.e. 'beautiful writing') does not interest me but I am excited about Good Writing. To me, what counts is not *what the letters look like*, but *which forces and movements were active in shaping the letters*.

The evolution of everyday cursives out of formal hands has been dominated by two tendencies: reducing the number of strokes required, and rounding the angles (E = 4 strokes, e = 1 stroke). Modern Hebrew cursive is plagued by too many slopes, and many characteristics are blurred. Can this be corrected?

Trial for a school model of a Hebrew everyday cursive

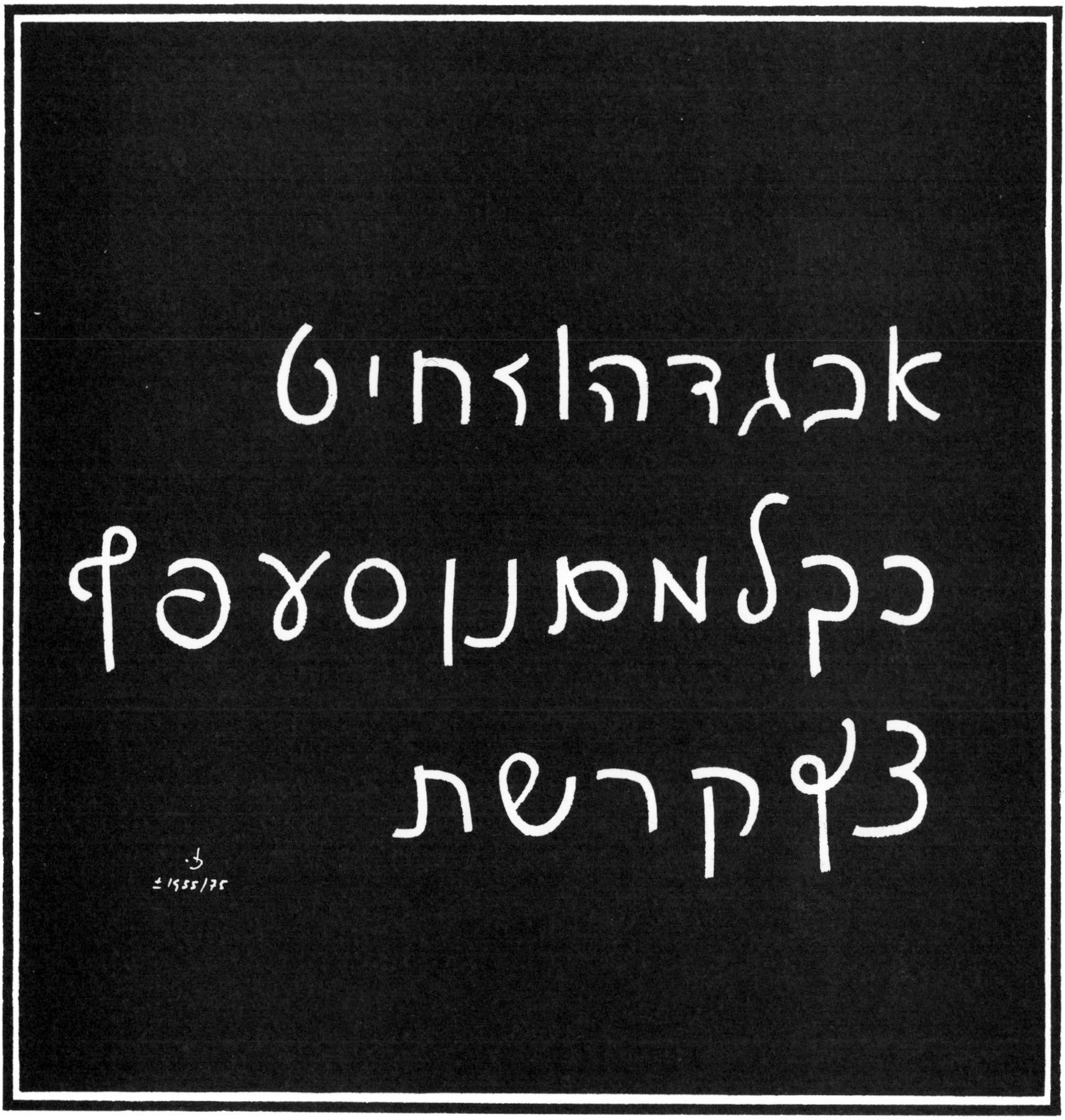

אבגדהוזחיט

כךלמםנןסעפף

צץקרשת

± 1955/75

Peter Halliday

26 Stapenhill Road
Burton on Trent
Staffordshire DE15 9AE

Peter Halliday was born in England in 1939 and studied writing, illuminating and lettering with Maisie Sherley at Medway College of Art in Rochester. He is Fellow of the Society of Scribes and Illuminators and was Chairman from 1982 to 1985. He teaches full-time at a high school in Staffordshire, where he is head of the Art Department, and has lectured and conducted workshops in England, Holland and the USA. In addition to many one-man and group exhibitions on both sides of the Atlantic he exhibited in 'The Art of the Scribe' exhibition in 1981, 'Calligraphy '84' and 'Lettering Arts in the '80s'. His work is represented in many private collections in the UK, Holland, Australia and USA, in the catalogue for 'Modern Scribes and Lettering Artists', 'Contemporary British Lettering', 'Calligraphy '84' and 'Lettering Arts in the '80s', as well as in *Graphics World* (October 1980), *Calligraphy Idea Exchange* (vol. 2, no. 4) and the new edition of the *Calligraphers' Handbook*.

He lives in the brewing capital of Britain, Burton on Trent, with his wife, three children, mother and cat in a large Victorian house in which the paintwork has been sacrificed to calligraphic endeavour.

Combined Free Roman and Uncial Alphabets
The freely written Modern Roman is an alphabet which I have been using since the '70s when I was experimenting and breaking away from more conventional calligraphy. It has changed and developed steadily and seems to owe something to various roman hands, particularly the Uncial of the fourth and fifth centuries. The uncial hand written here is a freely developed version of the exquisite writing to be found in the Stonyhurst Gospels (St Cuthbert's Gospels). It has been arrived at after very close observation of the manuscript in the British Museum.

3/50   Peter Halldoorf 85

David Harris

Stone House
10 The Strand
Topsham
Exeter EX3 OJB

David Harris is a lecturer at Exeter College of Art and Design, where he is responsible for teaching lettering in the Faculty of Design. He is the organizer of the now annual six-day lettering workshop held at Exeter every Easter (and which provided the original inspiration for *Sixty Alphabets*). The workshop provides facilities for a wide range of lettering activity, including cutting in wood and stone, glass engraving, mosaics, grit blasting, illumination, broad-edge and roman lettering. In addition to lecturing he is an accomplished type and lettering designer with a number of published typefaces to his credit. Before teaching at Exeter he worked as a designer and letterer in London where he had his own studio. He also has an adorable wife, four children, three of whom are tracing father's footsteps, and two grandchildren, plus – you've guessed it – a dog called Bella. His normally equable character is only ruffled by typefaces whose names begin with either 'H' or 'U'.

'Bella' Capitals
Why Bella? Well, as all the other members of the family have had a typeface named after them, only the dog was left. So should you see a beautiful beagle whose tail is inclined to finish in a fine flourish its name could be Snoopy . . . or Bella.

Michael Harvey

4 Valley Road
Bridport
Dorset DT6 4JR

Michael Harvey has been a professional lettering designer since 1955. After six years carving inscriptions for Reynolds Stone he became a designer of book jackets, typefaces, logotypes and architectural lettering. He is also a teacher of lettering and lecturer on both sides of the Atlantic, as well as being the author of two books, *Lettering Design* and *Creative Lettering*. His other interests include photography, jazz, and in the little spare time that he has, cycling and running.

Since the sixteenth century, scribes have produced sample alphabets as exemplars, or to impress customers and upstage rivals, and printers and type founders have published specimens of their products in alphabet form. These often beautifully conceived designs were essentially promotional material to generate commissions or business and not ends in themselves. The alphabet as an art object is a recent idea in which the abstract qualities of letters, their arrangement and material form are valued for their own sake.

    The lettering designer, freed from the considerations of meaning and language, is able to bring to an alphabet design some of the excitement he has experienced working with letters and feel, briefly, that he is an artist concerned solely with abstract form.

    In the design opposite, two alphabets are juxtaposed to create a dramatic effect, the formally arranged roman capitals thrust apart by the column of vigorous italic letters. There is an extra element provided by the fact that italic letters stand at the end of a long line of calligraphic development from roman capitals, and that even in this aggressive form the pen-derived strokes are still evident.

    In the production of this design stencils were cut for the italic alphabet, each copy being individually hand-stencilled with acrylic paint, while the capitals were drawn with a fibre-tipped pen and photocopied onto the paper. The stencil breaks, which add an extra interest to the italic letters, follow the original pen stroke sequence.

48

AB abc CD
EF defg GH
IJK hijk LM
N lmn OP
QR opqrs ST
UV stuv W
X wxyz YZ

Jost Hochuli

Waldgutstrasse 37
CH-9010 St Gallen

Born in St Gall in 1933, Jost Hochuli was trained at the Kunstgewerbeschule there from 1952 to 1955. He had his practical training at the printers Zollikofer AG, where he served an apprenticeship as a compositor from 1955 to 1958, during which time he attended courses at the Kunstgewerbeschule in Zurich. In 1958 he went to the Ecole Estienne in Paris. Since 1959 he has had his own studio in St Gall. He taught lettering part-time at the Zurich Kunstgewerbeschule from 1967 to 1980, and now teaches lettering and typography at the St Gall Kunstgewerbeschule.

My work has been described as simple and staid at first sight, but rich and complex on closer inspection: both cool and warm at the same time. This two-sidedness became more marked when I learned to know and appreciate typical exponents of dogmatic Swiss commercial graphics in the Swiss Arts & Crafts Society, while at the same time attending the lettering classes of Walter Käch. In this way I looked both backwards and forwards, as I still do, and would not like to do one without the other.

Karlgeorg Hoefer

Weilburger Weg 7
D-6050 Offenbach am Main

Karlgeorg Hoefer was born in 1914 and studied at the School of Arts and Crafts in Offenbach am Main with Professor Ernst Engel. From 1946 to his retirement in 1979 he was a teacher of lettering at the same school, and also a faculty member of the College of Design in Offenbach. He has done freelance work as a designer of typefaces as well as lettering design for various commercial projects. Since 1981 he has been giving calligraphy workshops in America and has become head of the calligraphy school at the Klingspor Museum, Offenbach.

Kalligrafie Etuden

Lothar Hoffmann

Domus Graphica
20927 Country Club
Harper Woods
Michigan 48225

Lothar Hoffmann was born in Germany. He studied in Berlin, Munich and Essen, before emigrating to the USA in 1964. He is Professor of Graphic Communications and Chairman of the Graphic Design Department at CCS in Detroit, Michigan. He has designed logos, catalogues and medical textbooks, and since 1976 has operated his own studio Domus Graphica. His calligraphy has been published in *International Calligraphy Today* and *Lettering Arts in the '80s*. He loves to work on his farm near Port Sanilac.

'Freude mit Buchstaben' (The Joy of Letters)
For almost two years I have been fascinated with a very simple writing instrument: a sharpened popsicle-stick. The simplicity and lack of flexibility are important ingredients. There are no cuts or slots for inkflow, no reservoir, and most of the time I work with Dr Martin's Dyes. The flat edge or corner of 'the stick', which I hold without any handle or grip, produces the most beautiful thick and thin lines. I am grateful to Robert Roesler of Dearborn, Michigan, who has developed the honing of popsicle-sticks into an art.

Lothar Hoffmann · 1985

David Howells

36 High Street
Kibworth Beauchamp
Leicester LE8 OHQ

David Howells is a Visiting Professor in Calligraphy to the Royal College of Art. He has been a Professor in Calligraphy and Letterform Design in the School of Graphic Design, Leicester Polytechnic, for thirty-one years, tutoring students for the BA and MA Honours Degrees in Graphic Design with a specialization in Calligraphy.

He teaches in the Society of Scribes and Illuminators summer school and conducts workshops in both Great Britain and the United States. He has travelled throughout Europe and has assembled an exceptional collection of slides on lettering which he uses for lectures and workshops.

During the 1930s and 1940s, while serving in the Royal Air Force, he travelled extensively in Egypt, Sudan, Eritrea and India. From 1948 to 1952 he studied at Brighton College of Art and Crafts, and was awarded the National Diploma in Design for Writing, Illuminating and Lettering and for Lithographic Illustration with distinction. In addition, he completed a fifth pedagogical year for the Ministry of Education Art Teacher's Diploma. In 1954 he was elected a Fellow of the Society of Scribes and Illuminators.

His calligraphy extends to editions of lithographs, private commissions and one-man exhibitions. Published work appears in *Calligraphy Today*, *Taplinger/Pentalic Engagement Calendars*, the exhibition catalogues *Art of the Scribe* and *Calligraphy '84*, and in *Modern Scribes and Lettering Artists*.

'Incidental Alphabets'

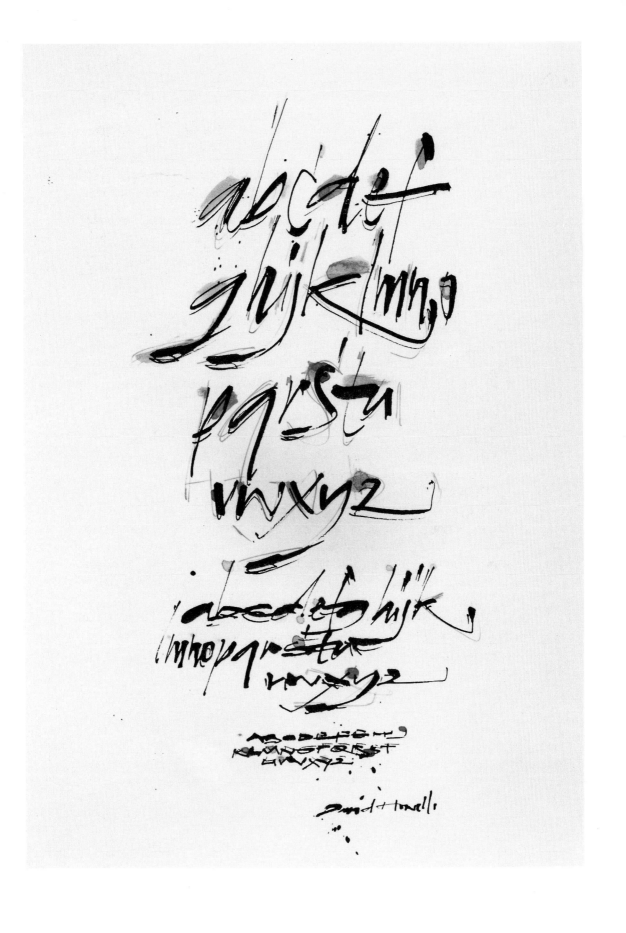

Nancy Ouchida Howells

36 High Street
Kibworth Beauchamp
Leicester LE8 OHQ

Nancy Ouchida Howells was awarded the Art Faculty Scholarship and graduated with a Master of Arts Degree in Design, specializing in Lettering, from California State University, Los Angeles. She combines a career in freelance graphic design and calligraphy; the Office of Ray and Charles Eames, IBM and Mazda Motors are among her clients. A Charter Member of the Society for Calligraphy and a former President of that group, Nancy has exhibited widely; her work was selected 'best of category' in calligraphy at Otis Parsons' 'Illustration West 19' Exhibition. She has taught privately in her studio for fifteen years and throughout the USA, and now in England where she lives with her husband.

10 April 1985

The air was still in the dusk. Large dark rain clouds threatened in the sky. The blades of grass sparkled and twinkled with the lace of raindrops. The naked tree branches were pushing forth their buds with a touch of green gracing each branch and stem. A line of great oaks stood tall, their branches reaching into the sky, while their feet were blanketed in a wave of golden daffodils.

The air was alive with the evening chorus: the chattering flocks of sparrows, the warning whistle and click-click of the blackbirds, the noisy fighting starlings, and the cheerful twittering song of the wren. Adding to the chorus were the occasional baas of the sheep and the almost baby-like cry of the lambs moving in a bouncy trot – their first steps in life. In the distance, I could hear the muffled ringing of the bells from our twelfth century village church; Wednesday night is the weekly rehearsal night of the eight bell ringers.

I feel that it is such a privilege and blessing to witness such life and beauty. The richness of life here is the inspiration from nature.

Written after a walk in the English countryside

Pam Jones

32 Sunnyside Road
Birnam
Johannesburg 2196

Pam Jones was born in Johannesburg in 1936. A lettering/display artist by profession, she runs her own studio business from home. Having taken up calligraphy three years ago, she studied with Joe Vasconcelles (President of the Calligraphy Society in South Africa) and became a committee member of the Calligraphy and Italic Society of South Africa, assisting in the production of the society's magazine. She recently participated in a very successful group calligraphy exhibition at the Johannesburg Public Library.

Alphabet executed with automatic pen and felt-tip marker on Conqueror Stock.

Torfi Jónsson

Þingholtsstraeti 17
Reykjavík

Torfi Jónsson studied graphics and design at the Hamburg Kunsthochschule from 1956 to 1961, where his main teachers were Professor Werner Bunz and Professor Sichowsky. From 1962 he taught graphics and design at the Arts and Crafts School in Reykjavík. During the same period he was also designing books and in 1978 he moved to Oslo to work as a book designer for the Norsk Korrespondanceskole-Forlag. Since 1982 he has been principal of the Arts and Crafts School in Reykjavík. His main interests are calligraphy and painting.

Jerry Kelly

A. Colish Inc.
40 Hartford Avenue
Mount Vernon
New York 10550

Jerry Kelly studied calligraphy with Denis Lund, Don Kunz and Hermann Zapf. He also has an interest in printing and fine books, and now works as a typographer at A. Colish Inc., in addition to being a partner at the Kelly/Winterton Press. His calligraphy and printing have been featured in several exhibitions.

There is A nothing B more useful C to the D E typographer F than the G study of the H history and I practice K of fine L writing. M Palpably N there O can be P no future R for the S typographer T who can U see no farther V than W the X typefounder's Y specimen. Z 1926

Stanley Morison

David Kindersley

152 Victoria Road
Cambridge CB4 3DZ

Born in 1915, David Kindersley is a self-employed stonecarver and designer of alphabets. From 1933 to 1936 he was apprenticed to Eric Gill. He taught at the Cambridge College of Arts and Technology (1946-57) and has been adviser to the Ministry of Transport on the lettering of street-names, adviser to the Shell Film Unit on design of titles, and consultant to Letraset International. He now runs his own workshop in Cambridge with Lida Lopes Cardozo.

Jean Larcher

16 Chemin des Bourgognes
95000 Cergy

Born in 1947 in Rennes, Jean Larcher studied lead typography and printing techniques from 1962 to 1965. At the same time, he took classes in calligraphy in a school run by the municipality of Paris. In 1973 he became a freelance typographic designer and calligrapher, also teaching typography, organizing exhibitions, writing articles and lecturing on the evolution of graphic design. Since the beginning of the 1980s he has begun to develop his activities as a creator of logotypes. Most recently, he has practised calligraphy purely as an art form – as a means of expression – and has participated in the 'revival' of this art especially in France, where the word 'calligraphie' was completely unknown twenty years ago. He travels frequently and has published several books, including *Calligraphies* (1984). In 1985 he published the first French calligraphic journal, entitled *Typomondo 5*.

This alphabet was originally drawn with the steel pen Speedball 3, black Chinese ink on white offset paper (37 x 60 cm) for the book *Calligraphies* published by Editions Quintette, Paris, in 1984.

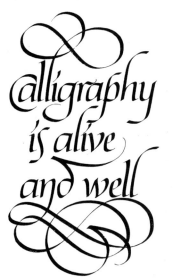

An original poster, published by the artist in 500 copies, printed in red. Written in black Chinese ink with the steel Automatic Pen 4 on Ingres d'Arches (32 x 56 cm). The design pays homage to the device of the Society of Scribes of New York City.

Lilly Lee

Unit 357
Clerkenwell Workshops
31 Clerkenwell Close
London EC1 0AT

Lilly Lee found herself at King's Cross railway station in the rain, broke, and with no roof over her head, and decided to take up calligraphy. She studied in England at the Digby Stuart College and subsequently, on being awarded a Crafts Council study grant, with Donald Jackson, Richard Kindersley and Sheila Waters. She has exhibited at the Society of Scribes and Illuminators (1981 and 1984) and the Manchester Craft Centre (1985). Her teaching posts have included the American College in London, the London College of Printing and West Dean College in Sussex. She was born in 1952 in Mesa, Arizona.

ABCDEF GHIJKLM NOPQRS TUVWXY Z

abcdefghijkl mnopors tuvwxyz

Alphabets · alphabets

Chuck Lehman

3519 SW California Street
Portland
Oregon 97219

Charles Lehman studied at Reed College, Portland, Oregon, with Lloyd Reynolds and Arnold Bank. He is concerned with research, design and development of handwriting education programmes and materials based on historically sound letterforms and writing techniques; he advocates the use of italic letterforms in basic handwriting programmes in schools and believes that the traditional craft philosophy and attitude of work are educationally essential for children today.

Lehman's publications include *Handwriting Models for Schools* (The Alcuin Press) and *Italic Handwriting & Calligraphy for Beginners* (Taplinger). He also privately publishes limited editions of low-cost books about the craft of calligraphy, under the banner of The Alcuin Press. The Alcuin booklist includes works by Reynolds, Fairbank, Ruskin and, most recently, a book entitled *Secreta* by Joyce Grafe.

He is currently administrator of curriculum at the Tigard Public School, Oregon.

Harry Meadows

The Spinney
Coed-y-Paen
Nr Pontypool
Gwent NP4 0SZ

Harry Meadows, NDD, ATD, FSSI, was born in 1931. He trained at the Newport College of Art and Design and the London University Institute of Education. He works freelance in calligraphy and letter-cutting.

'Gwent'
The alphabet was originally sketched and used for V-section incised cutting in the indigenous stone of Wales – slate. Revivals and adaptations of ancient forms give it an uncial character. Although designed for letter-cutting, the forms have been influenced by calligraphy and the broad-pen. It is named 'Gwent' after the Welsh border county where the designer was born and now practises. It is intended as one of a series of alphabets with geographical associations.

Karina Meister

Ten Kate Straat 65 ii
1053 BZ Amsterdam

Karina Meister was born in 1945 in Salzburg, Austria. From 1973 to 1978 she studied illustration and lettering at the Royal Academy of Art and Design at 's-Hertogenbosch, Netherlands. She worked for two years as a book designer and now teaches and is a freelance book designer and calligrapher.

'Bastarda', woodcut
Recently I did a woodcut title-page and initials for a letter of the composer Heinrich Schütz to be published in a private-press edition. For this purpose I again studied bastarda scripts and *civilité* type. I especially value its strong, tense abstract forms, the possibility of using various shapes of the same letter in one word, its capitals and lower-case fitting so well together.

The previous studies I did with a broad-edged reed, but with the techniques of woodcut in mind: I somewhat sharpened especially the round forms. To copy onto the woodblock I made an outline drawing. The cut finally did not satisfy me. I had to make changes and do it again.

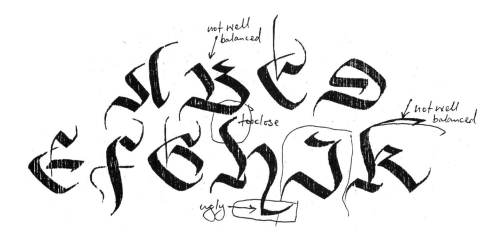

Merilyn Moss

9 Clotilda Court
Mill Valley
California 94941

Merilyn Moss has been working as a calligrapher in the San Francisco Bay Area since 1976. She likes little boys, particularly David Samson her six-year-old son. Painting with watercolours is one of her interests, along with collecting stones; tumbled chevron amethysts are her favourites. Lately she's been found exercising at the Nautilus Club, developing biceps as her portfolio was getting a bit heavy to carry.

'Aleph Bet II'
One challenge I enjoy is writing in a language that has unfamiliar characters. Hebrew is my favourite foreign alphabet. Actually it's not too terribly foreign since I am able to read it. It's simple, phonetic and straightforward, even though everyone seems to think it's truly backwards. I began by using a large brass pen to make solid letters. They were all done in two lines, arranged, then cut and pasted, moved and shifted. I glued my arrangement down and then traced outlines of what I had. More shifting around. Then it felt right and I did letter outlines onto watercolour paper with a big bamboo pen. I like Hebrew letters especially to look lively and cheerful. The letterforms themselves were quite classical and Ashkenazic in rendering. My favourite letter is the mem (מ). I coloured it in my favourite shade of coral pink.

Pat Musick

10 Studio Place
Colorado Springs
Colorado 80904

Pat Musick has worked as a window-dresser for an antiquarian bookshop; counsellor at a school for delinquents; visiting lecturer at the Central School of Art and Design for five years; freelance designer, letterer, enameller and tutor in these fields in America, England and Ireland for ten years. Her educational credentials include a BA in Art from Reed College, Portland, Oregon, and an M Phil from the Council for National Academic Awards/Central School of Art and Design, London. She also studied lettering at the Portland Art Museum School and the City and Guilds of London Art School under Lloyd Reynolds and Berthold Wolpe, respectively. Additional studies have included ceramics, writing, aikido, painting, American Indian culture, and wilderness skills. Her one surrogate child is a wolf/alsatian hybrid canine. She has a chronic phobia of simplistic thinking and isn't very rational at the prospect of running out of firewood either.

'Entropy'
The lettering grew out of many years' worth of looking at insular majuscule letterforms, in reproductions, original manuscripts, and inscriptions *in situ*; drawing the letters and counter shapes (freehand/traced; enlarged; accurate/ exaggerated); and writing the script with everything from quills, steel, paper and vellum to bamboo, sable, plaster and glass. The layout, influenced by the work of numerous twentieth-century scribes, developed out of several pen and pencil doodles. The piece became a vehicle for playing with some of the characteristics of insular lettering; repeating forms in counters, curved strokes, and wedge shapes; figure/ground ambiguity. Earlier sketches included letters that don't occur in original sources – j, k, v, w; modern y and g – but the 'tendency to greater randomness' seems to have precluded their appearance in the final design.

The immediate inspiration for this piece was the late arrival of the exhibition invitation and the occasion thus provided to try out one of the handmade papers from San Miguel Paper Workshop just down the road. Within forty-eight hours Tom Leech not only whipped up a batch of abaca paper but had the plate made, the edition printed, and remained enthusiastic about future collaborations, possibly involving welding.

80

Anne Yokosakamaki Okimoto

PO Box 10953
Costa Mesa
California 92627

Anne Okimoto first learned about calligraphy at Orange Coast College, Costa Mesa, and has since taken workshops, many at Calligraphic Arts (School, Supplies, Studio and Gallery), a calligraphy centre which she and her two lovely partners run. She is currently Special Projects Chairman for the Los Angeles Society for Calligraphy. Anne studies, freelances, teaches and dreams letterforms; to her, letters are like people in all their beauty, variety, complexity and challenge.

San Francisco – Japanese food – encouragement – music – freedom!

I am aware that this is 'lighthearted' but feel that in this area I am allowed to take liberties. The alternative would have been a 'quasi-Erté', for which I would never have been forgiven.

I live, dream, breathe and eat letterforms. When dieting, I consume few o's and q's and more l's.

Ronald Parsons

19 Grainger Close
Broadfields
Exeter EX2 5RL

Ronald Parsons trained in Exeter under Ruth Mary Wood, who was herself a pupil of Edward Johnston. He has work in Exeter Cathedral, Truro Cathedral, Buckfast Abbey and Lloyds Bank, as well as private collections and many churches and public buildings in Britain, Ireland, Africa and Yugoslavia. His preference is for Welsh and Cumbrian green slate but he works in a wide range of other stones from Britain and abroad. He also uses many different types of wood for lettered plaques, one of the favourite being laminated ash. Parsons is Chief Technician at the Exeter College of Art and Design and also works as a freelance designer, a civic and memorial lettercutter and a heraldic artist. He is also one of the course tutors for lettercutting at 'Lettering at Exeter' workshops (1984 and 1985).

Upper and lower case italic/roman drawn in pencil
I use these whenever possible because of the freedom they allow me.

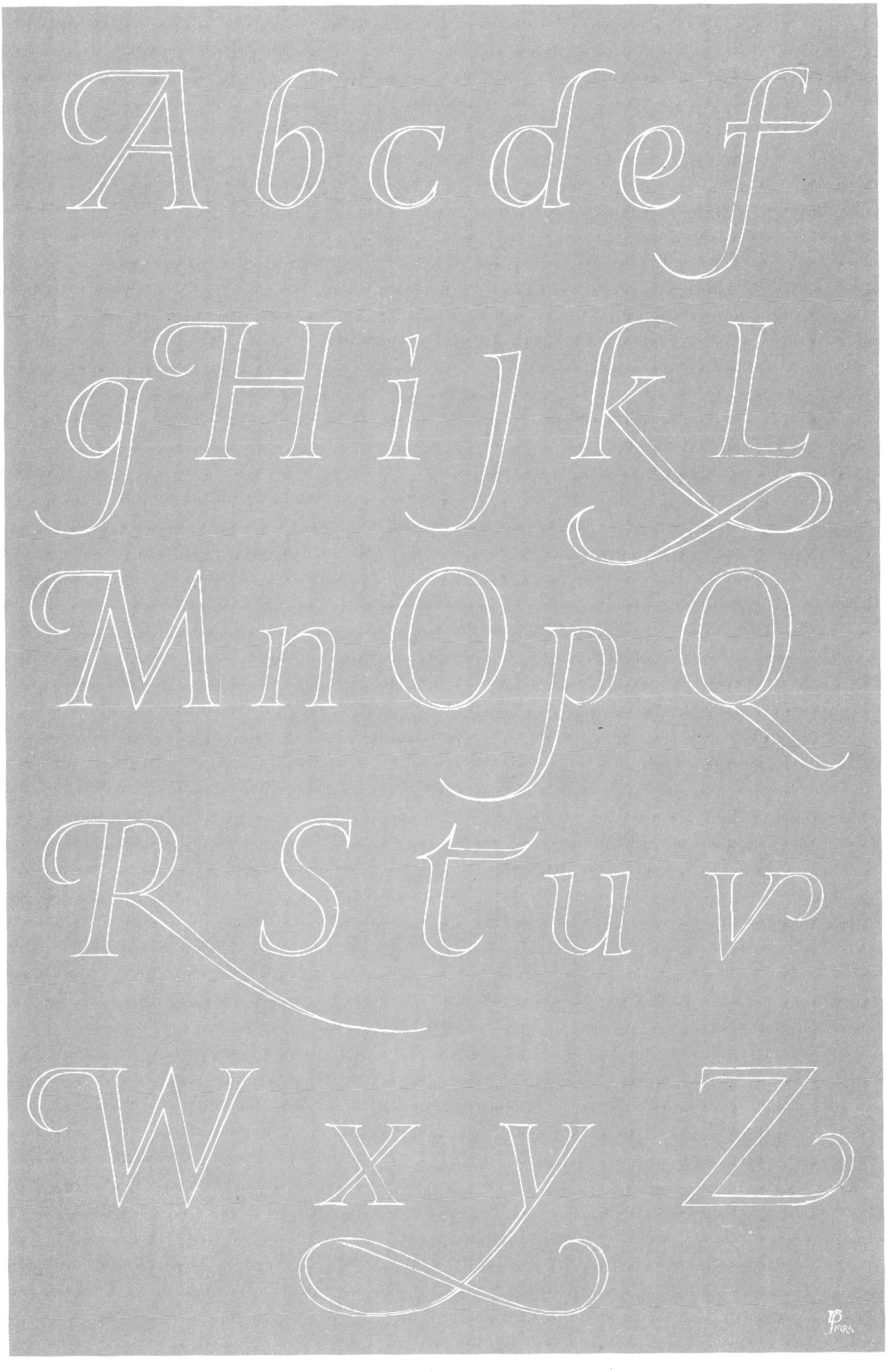

A b c d e f

g H i j k L

M n O p Q

R S t u v

W x y Z

Leonid Pronenko

350065 Krasnodar
Nevkipelova Street 15-67
USSR

Leonid Pronenko was born in 1939. After finishing secondary school in 1957 he took employment as a factory worker and as a freight handler as well as serving in the army. In 1965 he entered the Art Faculty of the Krasnodar University; after graduating he worked as a senior teacher. He began to teach himself calligraphy in 1977 and has exhibited locally, nationally and internationally. He is a member of the USSR Union of Artists.

David Quay

Quay & Gray Lettering Designers
11 Great Marlborough Street
London W1V 2ND

Born in 1948 in London, David Quay studied graphic design at Ravensbourne College of Art and Design. After leaving college he worked in various design groups before going freelance in 1975 to specialize in lettering. In 1983 he set up the lettering design consultancy of Quay & Gray in London, with partner Paul Gray, specializing in lettering and logotype design and more recently also magazine, book-jacket and general graphic design.

David Quay has also designed many alphabets. The work shown here led to a type that is available in Letraset and on most text photosetting systems. The typeface was inspired by the work of Frederick Goudy, and took nearly two years to develop. Although only roman capitals are shown here, all four weights have accompanying lower case and an italic. Initially only the two outer weights were drawn (light and bold); these were then digitalized onto computer and then, by using the Ikarus software program, the two interweights (book and medium) were produced. This was done in the Letraset Type Design Studio. Shown here are a selection of the different weights that are all completely computer generated.

David also spasmodically lectures on and teaches lettering design. His work has appeared regularly in international design magazines, annuals and exhibitions.

He is a member of The Society of Typographic Designers and The Type Directors Club of New York.

QUAY

ABCDE
FGHIJK
LMNOP
QRSTU
VWXYZ

ROMAN

Mohammed S Saggar

82 Galeries des Damiers
92400 Courbevoie
France

Mohammed S Saggar, who now lives and works in Paris, was born in Iraq in 1934. The creator of the Saggar Alphabet, he is also recognized as an innovator in the art of Arabic calligraphy. His work has been seen in major international exhibitions in France, the United States, Russia, Iraq, Egypt, England and Iceland. His commissioned works adorn important public buildings in the Middle East, such as the King Khalid Airport in Riyadh and the International Airport and Presidential Palace in Baghdad.

The alphabet of 'Naskhi' calligraphy.

Hans Schmidt

Heinrich-Heine-Strasse 27
60500 Offenbach am Main

Hans Schmidt was born in 1923 in Leipzig, where he also studied. He is active in Mainz and Offenbach as a book designer and teacher of typography and lettering. In his freelance work he is concerned with the development of letters that are only just legible and in recent years, above all, with three-dimensional lettering.

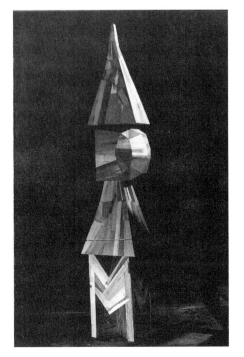

A
D
A
M – *letter sculpture, 1984,*
wood, height: 2.2m.

In the shadows of history stands ADAM. With him begins mankind, and therefore also the alphabet. The latter ends simply with Z; mankind ends and lies in the shadows of history, just like the beginning. Let us hope it doesn't end too soon with a bang.

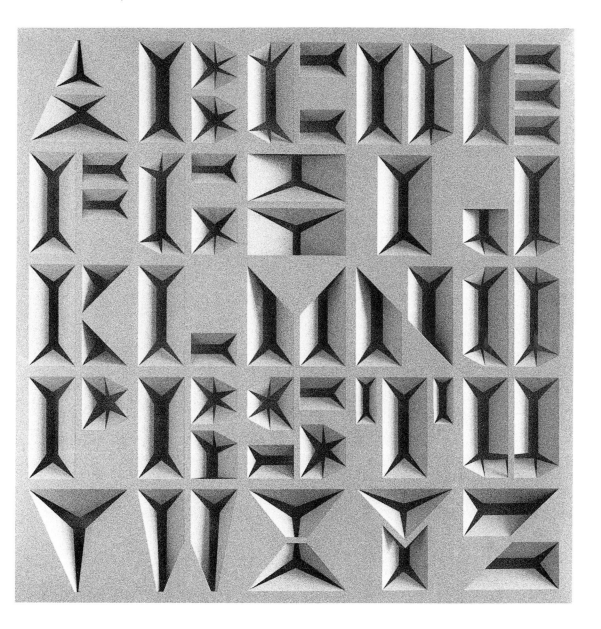

Werner Schneider

Am langen Land 2
D-5928 Bad Laasphe
Federal Republic of Germany

Werner Schneider is a widely celebrated designer of lettering and regularly contributes to major lettering exhibitions. He is a professor at the School of Design in Wiesbaden, where he also has a design studio.

Calligraphy breathes life. In my eyes it's an expression of my personal design. My works are spontaneous creations which lead me into a kind of visual adventure.

Writing-tools, papers and ink all play their part. Structures and contrasts in line have a special charm for me as they flow into expressive forms.

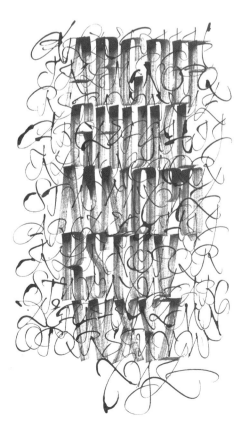

Written with a flexible pen with indian ink on Ingres paper. Freely written letters like these exploit the qualities of the pen and rely on many happy accidents.

94

Paul Shaw

110 Morningside Drive
New York
New York 10027

Paul Shaw is a freelance calligrapher and lettering artist. He teaches calligraphy, lettering and graphic design history at several universities and art schools in the New York City area. His work has been exhibited widely in the United States and he is the author of *Black Letter Primer* (Pentalic/Taplinger 1980; rev. ed., 1981). Trained as an historian he has received grants to research the work of type designer Morris Fuller Benton and calligrapher and book-jacket designer George Salter. Currently he is finishing a dissertation on the book and type designer W.A. Dwiggins at Columbia University. A member of the Board of Governors of the Society of Scribes Ltd, he resides in New York City.

I am fascinated by a wide variety of letterforms – whether calligraphic, typographic, drawn or otherwise created. The graphic design possibilities inherent in letterforms – the qualities of line, form, colour and texture – are my main concern. Thus, I have favourite *letters*, such as lower-case *a* and *g*, rather than favourite *alphabets*. The letters of our Roman alphabet, the alphabet of Western civilization, are like people in their infinite variety. Some are short and squat, others tall and slender; some run and caper about joyfully, others refuse to budge from their appointed places. Letters have a life of their own. As with people I admire those with perfect beauty, but I reserve my love for those with flaws, however small. Letters that are spontaneous, accidental, rough, sometimes even crude attract my attention and capture my lasting interest. Consequently, I have many influences, but the most important are: Rudolf Koch, F.H. Ernst Schneidler, George Salter, W.A. Dwiggins, A.M. Cassandre, Alfred Roller and Koloman Moser of the Vienna Secession, the poster artists of Art Nouveau and Art Deco, the Book of Kells, the French and Flemish scribes of the fifteenth century, Vincent Figgins, Bradbury Thompson and Piet Zwart.

John Smith

Tannenbaum
130 Gayton Road
King's Lynn
Norfolk PE30 4ER

John Smith studied at Cardiff College of Art, taking his NDD in Book Illustration and Lettercutting. Following an obligatory two years in the RAEC in Germany he taught pottery in Cardiff and later i/c Art at the Pontypool College of Further Education. He returned to Germany for nine years, teaching at King's School with the British Families Education Service, and then came back to the UK to lecture at the Mary Ward College of Education in Nottingham. He now lives in King's Lynn and lectures at the Norfolk College of Arts and Technology. He enjoys watercolour painting, photography and squash, is a compulsive hoarder and is mesmerized by old family photographs. He inscribed the lists of bishops and deans for Llandaff Cathedral and also the Victoria Cross Vellum for the Cathedral's Welch Regt. Chapel. He has frequently exhibited with the Society of Scribes and Illuminators and has had work published in Studio Vista's *Modern Scribes and Lettering Artists*. More recently he produced the calligraphic titles and credits for the BBC Television programme *Minstrel of the Dawn*.

'Alphascape'
The permutations of shapes and spaces that can be created by twenty-six letters hold a lifetime's design. Coupled with variations in size and the playing of positive against negative the potential is never-ending. But I am rarely satisfied.

Bonnie Spiegel

121 William Street
Portland
Maine 04103

Living in a large semi-Victorian house which she shares with her husband, two children, dog and two cats, Bonnie Spiegel works as an artist and teacher specializing in calligraphy. She holds a BFA degree from the Cooper Union School of Art in New York City where she, along with her entire freshman class, was introduced to calligraphy as part of the fine arts programme. She began her career as a book designer, but it wasn't until several years later when she left full-time employment and began freelancing that she began to seriously educate herself as a calligrapher. Beginning as an economic necessity – typesetting was too expensive – calligraphy quickly grew into the primary focus of her career when she discovered, to her delight, an eager and enthusiastic audience for her work. For the past three years she has been the editor of *Maine Pen and Ink*, a publication dealing with the lettering arts, which is sponsored by the Calligraphers of Maine, an organization she helped found. Her work is exhibited widely and can be seen in publications and collections both at home and abroad.

On Composing An Italic Boogie

Selecting an alphabet was the most difficult part of designing this piece. I like so many. But in the end I had to keep to the italic hand, my first love in my affair with letters and still my hands-down favourite. Using italic, I could show the excitement I feel when I letter. Italic also has the potential for both the energy and grace that I want in my work.

This piece is a silkscreened print of an alphabet collage. After writing at least a thousand alphabets with my five-line pen, I selected one to use as a basis for the finished piece. Then I began to play, using the other 999 as raw material. I cut out parts, finding letter-shapes and parts of letters that I could use to enhance the structure or increase the textural contrast or create a greater flow of movement and energy. Sometimes I would draw more shapes or add a line or two. I did whatever was necessary to complete the piece to my satisfaction.

100

John Stevens

18 Manor Place
Huntington Station
New York 11746

John Stevens is a calligrapher, lettering artist and signwriter, living and working in Huntington, New York. Originally his background was as a signwriter, but since 1979 he has pursued his interest in the calligraphic arts, learning mostly from books and some workshops.

He was an instructor at the Minnesota Conference in 1984 (where he won an MMI award) and at the conference in Los Angeles in 1985. His work is in both public and private collections throughout the US and elsewhere and has been featured in several calligraphic journals. Most recently he was awarded inclusion in the Type Directors' Show for calligraphic and design excellence.

'Slightly modified uncial'
This alphabet – I wouldn't call it my favourite – is one of many. The many being an ongoing dialogue I have with paper, ink, mood etc. Why alphabets? is usually the question. Although I do quotations, logo designs, signs, book titles and lettering for the more utilitarian purposes, I continue to do alphabets because unlike those other activities of lettering, alphabets allow me the freedom to be totally expressive without regard to word content, legibility, client bias, typos, budget, authenticity, subject-matter etc. Just me and the formal elements of our art. It is truly amazing what can be done (as countless calligraphers already know) with just writing tool, paper and twenty-six characters. *Calligraphic Hedonism* could be the subtitle of this book. But I wouldn't consider this activity a petty indulgence; rather an extremely high form of expression which also happens to be a visual vocabulary builder that can do the mundane work no harm.

John Stevens 1985

Alan Swanson

Asst Professor of Scandinavian and Comparative Literature
Brigham Young University
Provo
Utah 84602

Alan Swanson endeavours to learn how to make an S properly. As this will surely take the rest of his life, he must also, for his sins, teach comparative literature. The powerful ghost of Edward Catich hovers over him, however, reminding him always to 'practise, practise, practise'.

Catich's legacy in my work is indeed strong. The pangram about frowzy things is his composition and is one of the few perfect ones in English. Furthermore, his long-standing interest in the Trajan inscription and Imperial Roman letters has made its mark on me. I thought it might be interesting to see what would happen with letters that aren't there.

Villu Toots

A. Kapi 6-10
Tallinn 200 031
Estonia
USSR

Villu Toots, the Estonian calligrapher and book artist, was born in Tallinn in 1916. He studied in Tartu, worked as a cinema artist and during the post-war years as an art director at a publishing house. Since 1952 he has practised as a freelance artist. In 1965 he founded a Lettering Art School, whose graduates include some of the leading Estonian calligraphers. He has organized major exhibitions and symposia on lettering and calligraphy both in Estonia and in other republics.

Villu Toots is married, has one daughter and three grandchildren. He is the head of the book artists branch of the Estonian League of Artists. In 1971 he was elected honorary member of the Society of Scribes and Illuminators and corresponding member of the Society of West German Book Artists. His work has been reproduced in many publications and he himself has written eight books on lettering, as well as lecturing on the subject both in the Soviet Union and abroad.

There cannot be nice books without nice lettering, nor a high culture without nice books.

I belong to those people who enjoy making letters and designing lettering, the aesthetic impact of which overshadows their communicative value. Curiously enough, in my native language one and the same word stands for both 'star' and 'letter'. In this way, I have been a star-gazer throughout my conscious life, and letters have been my guiding stars in the choice of my profession. Ever since my schooldays I have been contemplating letters *with my own eyes*, making letters *at my own will*. The noble ancient art of lettering has become my life, my work and my hobby.

The first good book I could acquire was *Lettering of Today* (1937). Its study was a turning-point for me; a self-taught letterer, I started to revise my work and my principles. I was greatly attracted by the endeavours of Edward Johnston and his school; I still hold him in high esteem, though now I consider myself a representative of the more liberal wing of his school.

Mark Van Stone

276 State Street
Portsmouth
New Hampshire 03801

While studying Babylonian mathematical tablets in 1969, Mark Van Stone discovered that the artistry of cuneiform writing intrigued him much more than the content. Thus began a ceaseless study of written forms for which his university sent him to Irish and English libraries to study the Book of Kells and its kin. In spite of this, he took his degree in physics. He is a very popular teacher, among scribes and medieval scholars, travelling widely to instruct, exhibit and lecture on the techniques of medieval manuscript production. In 1982-3 he spent several months studying netsuke carving, and learning to see, in Japan. He presently resides in Portsmouth, New Hampshire, where he publishes *U&lhu*, a satirical calligraphy newsletter, writes and carves, builds sandcastles, and organizes exhibitions and other schemes designed to raise the world's consciousness of the letter arts.

An illuminated alphabet, each letter in a different style, in roughly chronological order. The A is fourth-century Italy, the Z is sixteenth-century Holbein. Only the H and Q are direct copies, the others are all inventions of the artist, but in historic styles, the identification of which is left as an exercise to the student. Sufficient space for the explanation does not exist in the present format.

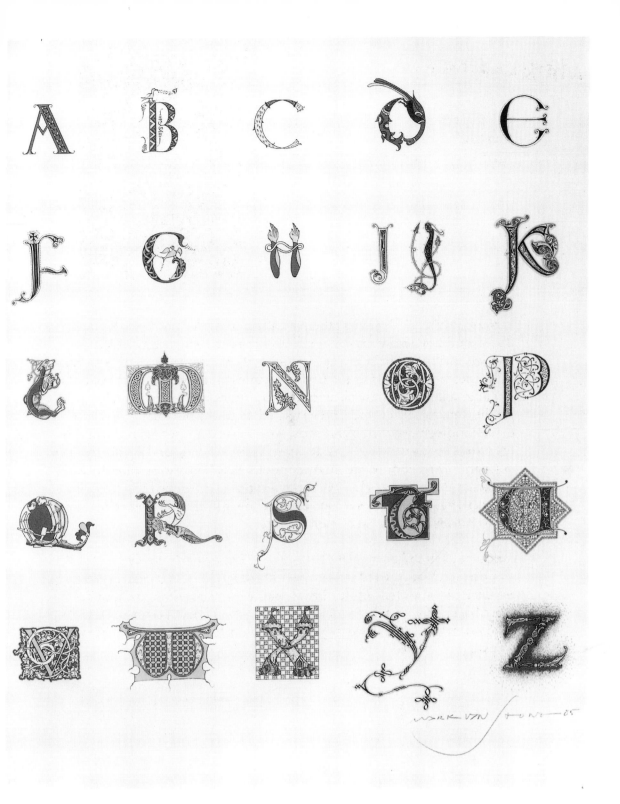

MARK VAN STONE 05

Jovica Veljović

Gospodara Vučića 229
11000 Belgrade

Born in 1954 at Suvi Do in Yugoslavia, Jovica Veljović studied at the Academy of Applied Art in Belgrade where he specialized in lettering and calligraphy. He works as a calligrapher and type designer and now has a freelance kitchen for alphabet soups in Belgrade.

This is a Serbian alphabet (Srpska ćirilica) which consists of thirty characters. The six letters marked with an asterisk exist only in Serbian Cyrillic, so be careful – keep away!

I made another piece much better than this one, but my son threw his ball on it before it was completely dry. I wanted to squeeze him, but he seriously and quietly told me; 'Daddy, Briem deserves a much better piece than this – try again!' So here it is.

Greeting card

ЖЕЛИМО · ДА · ВАС · НЕ · БОЛИ · ОНО · ШТО
ВАС · ЈЕ · БОЛЕЛО · И · ДА · ВАС · ВОЛИ · СВЕ
ОНО · ШТО · ВАС · ЈОШ · НИЈЕ · ВОЛЕЛО ·

ЖЕЛИМО · ДА · ВАМ · ДЕЦА · БУДУ · БОЉА
ОД · ВАС · ДА · СЕ · ВИШЕ · ВИ · ХВАЛИТЕ
ЊИМА · НЕГО · ОНИ · ВАМА ·

ЖЕЛИМО · ДА · ВАС · ДОБРО · СЛУЖЕ · НОГЕ
ДА · НА · ЊИМА · ПРОВЕДЕТЕ · ВЕЋИ
ДЕО · НОВЕ · ГОДИНЕ · ДА · ИМАТЕ
ВИШЕ · ПОСЛА · НЕГО · ВРЕМЕНА ·

ЖЕЛИМО · ВАМ · ДА · БУДЕТЕ · ПОТЗЕБНИЈИ
ДРУГИМА · НЕГО · ОНИ · ВАМА · ДА
ЖЕЛИТЕ · И · МОЖЕТЕ · ВИШЕ · НЕГО
ШТО · ВАМ · ТРЕБА · И · ДА · СВЕ · ШТО · ВАМ
ПРЕТЕКНЕ · ПОДЕЛИТЕ · СА · ОНИМА
КОЈИ · НЕ · МОГУ · КОЛИКО · ВИ ·

ЖЕЛИМО · НА · КРАЈУ · ДА · ОВА · ГОДИНА
ИМА · ВИШЕ · СРЕЋЕ · СА · ВАМА
НЕГО · ПРЕТХОДНА!   А · РАДОВИЋ

110

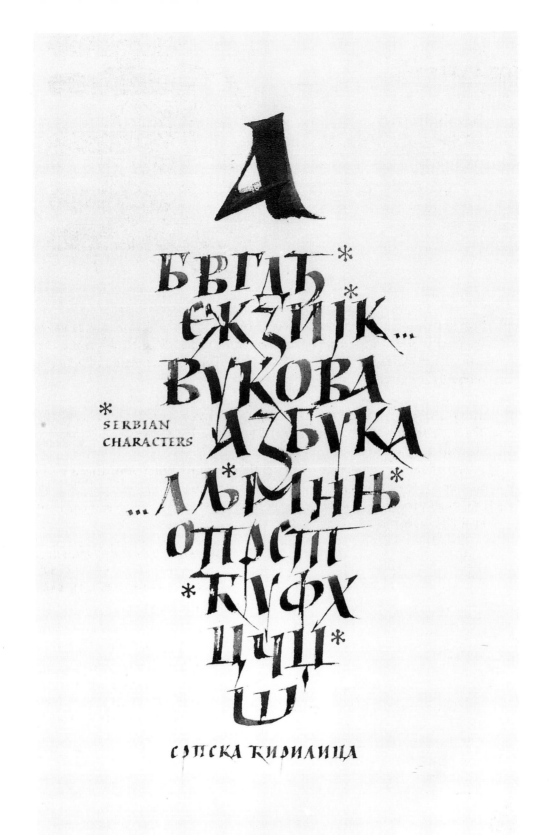

SERBIAN
CHARACTERS

СРПСКА ЋИРИЛИЦА

Julian Waters

9423 Gentle Circle
Gaithersburg
Maryland 20879

Julian Waters was born in England in 1957, and is now living and working in Washington DC. His works are represented in several calligraphic calendars and textbooks. He specializes in lettering and calligraphy for reproduction and typographic design for books and other publications. His clients include: Smithsonian Books, Library of Congress, the American Red Cross, University of Maryland, General Electric, and *National Geographic, New York* and *National Wildlife* magazines. He has supervised workshops throughout the US, Canada and Puerto Rico and has presented lectures for the Corcoran School of Art, The Typophiles (New York) and the Washington Art Directors Club, among others. He has also appeared at the international calligraphy conferences in Philadelphia (1982), Chicago (1983) and Los Angeles (1985).

   Julian's parents, Sheila and Peter Waters, are internationally known in their own fields of calligraphy, bookbinding and conservation and have both been helpful in his development. Julian studies fine arts and graphic design at Montgomery College, Maryland, and has studied lettering and type design with Hermann Zapf. In 1984 Julian Waters was asked to substitute for Professor Zapf, and teach a two-week advanced course in lettering at Rochester Institute of Technology.

'Contrasts'
This electrostatic print was made on mid-toned Fabriano paper with hand shading with white pencil. The *contrasts* are apparent almost everywhere. In size, texture, formality, thick/thin proportion, speed of technique etc. The top arrangement was a quick spontaneous doodle on watercolour paper with a tool made from rolled-up newsprint paper and the serifed forms were done on bond paper with a sharpened steel nib. The only thing that ties them together is the fact that they are both examples of roman capitals.

ABCDEFGHIJKLMNO
PQRSTUVWXYZ

Sheila Waters

20740 Warfield Court
Gaithersburg
Maryland 20879

Sheila Waters is an internationally known calligraphic artist. Her work is owned by royalty, museums, libraries, institutions and private collectors and has been exhibited widely. It is represented in most of the important books in the calligraphic literature. Born in England and trained at the Royal College of Art, she moved to the USA in 1971 with her husband, Peter (who is Conservation Officer at the Library of Congress), and their three sons Julian, Michael and Christopher. In 1972 she began the calligraphic programme for the Smithsonian Institution's Associates, has since given workshops and lectures extensively throughout the USA and Canada (receiving honorary memberships from several societies) and was founding president of the Washington Calligraphers Guild. 1981 marked the milestone of thirty years as an elected fellow of the prestigious London Society of Scribes and Illuminators, and also her inclusion in the *World Who's Who of Women*.

'Decorated Alphabet'
The 'Decorated Alphabet' is linked to the 'Roundel of the Seasons', a major project that in turn stemmed from my illuminated manuscript of Dylan Thomas' play *Under Milk Wood*. The alphabet makes a kind of bridge between the title-page of *Under Milk Wood* (when I first used these capitals) and the Roundel. All three show a preoccupation with letters having decoration within and between them.

Eleanor Winters

245 Warren Street
Brooklyn
New York 11201

Eleanor Winters is a commercial artist living and working in New York City. She teaches at the Calligraphy Workshop and travels widely, teaching workshops on a variety of calligraphic styles and applications, ranging from Copperplate to Calligrams, Foundational to Signwriting. She has edited *The Calligraphers Engagement Calendar* (Taplinger Publishing Co.) for the past five years, and her italic how-to book, *Calligraphy in Ten Easy Lessons* (Simon & Schuster) was published in 1984. She has been on the faculty of the International Calligraphy Conferences in Los Angeles, Chicago and Philadelphia.

'Ampersand'
This piece resulted from the marriage of my favourite hand, Gothicized Italic (based on Edward Johnston's compressed Pointed Italic) with my favourite symbol, the ampersand. The quest for an ampersand that would combine the blackletter qualities of the gothic part of Gothicized Italic, with the curvilinear forms of italic, resulted in piles of sketches, scribbles, trials and (mainly) errors. The transition from the spontaneity of the chosen sketches to an acceptably rendered finished form was the most difficult part of the process. The prints were made by offset on Stonehenge paper. The 'z' was added afterwards in gouache.

abbbcddeffgghhijjkkllmnoppqqrrsstuvvuwwxyyy

z

Berthold L Wolpe

110 Kennington Park Road
London SE11

Berthold L. Wolpe RDI has done many things in his time. He always designs first and measures afterwards.

I set my students at the City and Guilds of London Art School the task of modelling a plaque in terracotta clay and I cut this one at the same time. The clay is leather-hard when worked on and becomes as hard as brick after firing.

118

James Wood

530 Rosemarie Drive
Arcadia
California 91006

Jim Wood was born and raised in Los Angeles and received his art education at Frank Wiggins' trade school and Chouinard Art Institute. He worked for over forty years for advertising to sell wine, soap, foods, Chevrolets, Edsels, airlines, records and motion pictures. He taught classes in letterforms for nine years at Chouinard, and worked with the late George Stevens on his film *The Greatest Story Ever Told*. His privilege was to circulate with men of letters: Grant Dahlstrom, Hermann Zapf, Marty Oberstein, Ray Bradbury, Maury Nemoy, Mort Leach, Saul Bass, Ken Parkhurst and Arnold Bank. He married and produced two children, who begat three grandchildren, and now lives in the little town of Arcadia.

'Chancery'

I'll call this piece 'Chancery' just because it is the alphabet that got me hooked when I first noticed Oscar Ogg and attended an early lecture by Arnold Bank. The whole idea was the spirit of the letters; I had been restricted by art directors into drawing headlines for advertisements, and penmanship was pure fun; just like watercolours. So when I wrote the italic minuscules, it was with a Witch pen and fluid ink. The choice was from a half-dozen samples, and I picked one most art directors wouldn't like; a new criterion for selection.

The writing of
letters is an art
practiced by scribes
for hundreds of
years, and basic
letterforms, written
with the broad pen
have been
the method of
communication
and the model for
typefaces because of
their agreed forms
and the legibility of
their many
transitions:

Written with Mitchell Witch pen and Osmiroid nib
on Brienfang Bond by James L Wood in May 1982

Lili Cassel Wronker

144-44 Village Road
Jamaica
New York 11435

Born in Europe, Lili Cassel Wronker was introduced to Edward Johnston's *Writing & Illuminating & Lettering* at a high school in New York City. Her strongest influences came from the guidance of Robert Russin, Dr Robert Leslie, Arnold Bank, William Metzig and Donald Jackson.

She has illustrated children's books, designed book jackets, maps, labels, calendars, brochures, magazine headings, greeting cards, gravestones, taught calligraphy, and travelled extensively in the US, Europe and Israel.

She has an obsession about the spacing of i's.

She and her husband jointly operate a private handpress as a hobby.

My favourite alphabets were inspired by a sephardic fourteenth-century Hebrew and fifth/sixth century uncial because of the natural way the forms flow out of the flat-edged pen. The Hebrew has only twenty-two characters but five final letters were added. Both alphabets have only a few ascenders and descenders. The alphabets were written with Coit and Speedball C nibs, left-handed for the Hebrew. The prints are colour Xeroxes.

122

Hermann Zapf

Seitersweg 35
D-6100 Darmstadt

Hermann Zapf was born in Nuremberg in 1918. He received no art school training, learning calligraphy from books by Edward Johnston and Rudolf Koch. Besides calligraphy his main work is connected with the design of typefaces, such as Palatino, Optima etc., and with book design. He is an honorary member of the Society of Scribes and Illuminators, London.

Gudrun Zapf von Hesse

Seitersweg 35
D-6100 Darmstadt

Gudrun Zapf-von Hesse is a bookbinder, calligrapher and type designer. She has taught at the Staedel Art School in Frankfurt am Main. For the Stempel type foundry in Frankfurt she designed the Diotima and Smaragd typefaces, and the Ariadne initials, as well as Shakespeare roman and italic and a special typeface for photocomposition for Hallmark Cards Inc., Kansas City, Missouri. Born in Schwerin she now lives in Darmstadt.

A pen study for the italic of 'Diotima', the typeface used in this book.

Le Bonheur de ce Monde
SONNET

Avoir une maison commode, propre et belle,
Un jardin tapissé d'espaliers odorans,
Des fruits, d'excellent vin, peu de train, peu d'enfans,
Posseder seul, sans bruit, une femme fidéle.

N'avoir dettes, amour, ni procés, ni querelle,
Ni de partage à faire avecque ses parens,
Se contenter de peu, n'espérer rien des Grands,
Régler tous ses desseins sur un juste modéle.

Vivre avecque franchise et sans ambition,
S'adonner sans scrupule à la dévotion,
Domter ses passions, les rendre obéissantes.

Conserver l'esprit, et le jugement fort,
Dire son Chapelet en cultivant ses entes,
C'est attendre chez soi bien doucement la mort.

CHRISTOPHE PLANTIN

Diotima

Gudrun Zapf-von Hesse

ABCDEFGHIJKLMNO
PQRSTUVWXYZ
abcdefghijklmnopqrstu
vwxyz   12345 & 67890

ABCDEFGHIJKLMNO
PQRSTUVWXYZ
abcdefghijklmnopqrstuvwx
yz & ff tz   1234567890

D. Stempel AG   »Diotima-Kursiv«

This book is to be returned on or before
the last date stamped below.